Walking the Way
of the Cross

Julien Chilcott-Monk is a writer and musician living in
Winchester. He is the author of *A Basic Dictionary of Bible People*
and co-author, with Bishop Geoffrey Rowell, of *Come, Lord
Jesus* and *Flesh, Bone, Wood*.

WALKING THE WAY
OF THE CROSS

*Meditations on the Stations of the Cross for
personal and public devotion*

Julien Chilcott-Monk

Foreword by the Duke and Duchess of Norfolk

TUFTON
BOOKS

© Julien Chilcott-Monk 2005

First published in 2005 for Tufton Books
by the Canterbury Press Norwich
(a publishing imprint of Hymns Ancient & Modern Limited,
a registered charity)
St Mary's Works, St Mary's Plain,
Norwich, Norfolk, NR3 3BH

www.scm-canterburypress.co.uk

British Library Cataloguing in Publication data

A catalogue record for this book is available
from the British Library

ISBN 1-85191-049-1

Typeset in Perpetua by Regent Typesetting, London
Printed and bound by
Biddles Ltd, www.biddles.co.uk

CONTENTS

ACKNOWLEDGEMENTS

The illustrations of the Westminster Cathedral stations are reproduced by courtesy of The Administrator, Westminster Cathedral, and I am most grateful to Barry Palmer, the General Manager of the Cathedral, for making all necessary arrangements.

Scriptural quotations are from the Catholic Edition copyright 1965 and 1966 of the Revised Standard Version of the Holy Bible copyright 1946, 1952 and 1957 by the Division of Christian Education of the National Council of Churches in the USA, and are used by permission. All Rights Reserved.

To Father Richard Duffield
in gratitude

FOREWORD
by the
Duke and Duchess of Norfolk

It is rare to come across a devotional work designed for both private and public use. Here we have just such a book, with private and public forms for praying the Stations of the Cross using either the illustrations provided in the book or the Stations on the walls of our churches. We can pray this devotion while walking the Way of the Cross, while kneeling in the presence of the Blessed Sacrament, or while sitting in an armchair beside a crucifix.

The illustrations are reproduced from Eric Gill's superb sculptures in Westminster Cathedral, and Julien Chilcott-Monk guides us on the path towards seeing more clearly and understanding more fully Gill's powerful and subtle art, leading our imagination into deeper contemplation of the Passion of our Lord.

Walking the Way of the Cross is a book for use throughout the year; a book for every bookshelf, for every prie-dieu. We found it to be a truly beautiful, spiritual piece of work.

Edward and Georgina Norfolk

INTRODUCTION AND
HOW TO USE THE BOOK

Eric Gill's fourteen masterly sculptures of the Stations of the Cross have something of an ancient simplicity; they have contemporary appeal; they are laden with attitudes, gestures and juxtapositions of significance for those with patience to discern them. In Part 1 of this book, I have attempted to draw out some of these things; but the pilgrim in careful contemplation will find many more. These are simply the keys that will allow further and deeper exploration.

Eric Gill (1882–1940) was received into the Catholic Church on his birthday, 22 February 1913. In the summer of the same year, having been asked to do so, he began to sketch his ideas for the Westminster Cathedral stations. By the end of April the following year he had been commissioned to do the work. Curiously, the first station he tackled was the tenth, *Jesus is Stripped of His Clothes*, then the second, *Jesus Receives His Cross*, followed by the thirteenth, *The Body of Jesus is Taken from the Cross and Laid in Mary's Bosom*; and the last was the eleventh, *Jesus is Nailed to the Cross*. All fourteen were complete and in place by March 1918.

Many critics of the time, and since, have given praise to Gill only for his technical achievement and skilful execution. It is difficult to understand how the almost overwhelming profundity of his artistry revealed in these stations passed them by. It is surely there for those with eyes to see.

This master craftsman and artist has left us a large body of splendid work, but, I submit, no part of it finer than the stations. They are of the highest technical quality and, artistically, they can take us above and beyond fourteen isolated incidents in the journey from Gabbatha to Golgotha.

In Part 1 there are static or sedentary versions of the stations devotion for both the private pilgrim and for corporate pilgrimage, using illustrations of the Gill sculptures for reference. The text for the private pilgrim's devotion is supplied in italics before and after the meditations. In Part 2 there are versions for use with the stations provided in church, for both the private pilgrim and for corporate pilgrimage. Again, the text for the private pilgrim's devotion is supplied in italics before and after the meditations. In both Parts 1 and 2 a fifteenth station is given for use outside the penitential seasons. A shorter form of the stations devotion – ten stations only – omits stations IV, VI, VII, IX.

The stations devotion ought to begin and end in the presence of the Blessed Sacrament. For the static forms, the pilgrim(s) ought to remain in the presence of the Blessed Sacrament. For Lenten use, the fourteen stations may be used in three cycles of fourteen days throughout Lent in order to encourage the pilgrim to enter more deeply into the mysteries of the Passion of our Lord. Psalms and verses from Lamentations customarily associated with the Passion of our Lord are provided in each case to add other voices and perspectives to the devotion and meditation. Praying the stations ought to be as emotional an experience as actually setting foot along the Via Crucis in Jerusalem around two thousand years ago, which is aided, in Part 1, by the imagination and insight of Gill's carving. To pray the stations fully, the pilgrim ought to give his mind free rein when using the meditations, pausing awhile after each paragraph. However, this approach will not always be possible or appropriate when the conducted forms of the devotion are used.

All scriptural quotations are from the Catholic Edition of the Revised Standard Version of the Holy Bible, except in one or two places, because the RSV is probably still the best available translation. Furthermore, it reads well, and as neither Catholic nor Anglican customarily uses this translation at Mass, or probably in private devotion, it is perhaps a good idea to use a less familiar translation.

The history of the stations as a devotional exercise begins in the early centuries, when pious Christians made the journey to Jerusalem in order to walk in the steps of Christ along the Via Crucis, the Via Dolorosa.

By the beginning of the second millennium it was becoming an increasingly dangerous pilgrimage, and there arose the practice of erecting pictures of the journey to Golgotha in churches in southern Europe – at first in Spain, then at the hands of the Franciscan Minorites in mid-fourteenth-century Italy. The custom spread throughout Europe and elsewhere, and by the nineteenth century the fourteen stations, as we now know them, were well established, though during the evolution of the devotion any number between ten and sixteen was known.

Of course, the fourteen stages of the journey usually depicted are not all recorded in the canonical gospels. The three falls are not recorded, though the first may be surmised from the fact that Simon of Cyrene was detailed to carry the cross. And the synoptic gospels tell us that Simon of Cyrene *carried* the cross. Neither the meeting with Mary nor with Veronica is recorded in the gospels, but the meeting with Mary is certainly a reasonable leap to take. (A story about Veronica appears in the 'Acts of Pilate' and imagining an encounter on the Via Crucis is not too remote, and sits well within the fourteen stations. Some traditions tell us that Veronica was the woman whose issue of blood was cured in Luke 8.43–48.)

Whatever the stations and however we use them they give us a wonderful opportunity to contemplate, exercise and examine ourselves on the way to Golgotha.

Julien Chilcott-Monk
Michaelmas 2004

A visit to Westminster Cathedral to view the stations in situ is recommended. Gill's life is ably documented in the biography *The Life of Eric Gill* by Robert Speaight published by Methuen in 1966.

PART 1
STATIONS OF THE CROSS
FOR PERSONAL AND
PUBLIC DEVOTION

Using illustrations of Eric Gill's sculptures

*(The text in italics before and after the meditations is for
the use of the private pilgrim)*

✠
✠ ✠ ✠
✠
✠

PREPARATION
FOR PERSONAL DEVOTION

✠
✠ ✠ ✠
✠

+ *In the name of the Father, and of the Son, and of the Holy Spirit. Amen.*

O Lord Jesus, have mercy upon me and upon your whole Church living and departed. As I trace and meditate on the Way of the Cross, may I share in the merits of your Passion and may my heart be touched with sorrow and repentance that I may be ready to embrace with joy the sufferings and humiliations in my life and pilgrimage.

O Lord, come to me and help me.

[Glory be to the Father, and to the Son, and to the Holy Spirit. As it was in the beginning is now and ever shall be, world without end. Amen.]

PREPARATION
FOR PUBLIC DEVOTION

✠
✠ ✠ ✠
✠

Officiant	+ In the name of the Father, and of the Son, and of the Holy Spirit.
Pilgrims	**Amen.**
Officiant	Let us pray:
	O Heavenly Father and ever-living God, help us to be more faithful in our petitions and thanksgivings; more magnanimous and generous in our charitable acts; more diligent in celebrating the sacred mysteries through which we are reborn; and by doing so to come to the fullness of your heavenly grace. Through Jesus Christ our Lord, who lives and reigns with you and the Holy Spirit, one God through all the ages.
Pilgrims	**Amen.**
Officiant	+ Our help stands in the name of the Lord.
Pilgrims	**Who has made heaven and earth.**
[*Officiant*	Glory be to the Father, and to the Son, and to the Holy Spirit.
Pilgrims	**As it was in the beginning is now and ever shall be, world without end. Amen.**]
Officiant	Let us now consider the stations of the Passion of our Lord.

I

JESUS IS CONDEMNED TO DEATH

✠
✠ ✠ ✠
✠

He who dwells in the shelter of the Most High, who abides in the shadow of the Almighty, will say to the Lord, 'My refuge and my fortress; my God, in whom I trust.'

Psalm 91.1—2

✠

Officiant	My God, my God, why hast thou forsaken me?
Pilgrims	**Why art thou so far from helping me, from the words of my groaning?**
Officiant	O my God, I cry by day but thou dost not answer;
Pilgrims	**And by night, but find no rest.**
Officiant	Yet thou art holy,
Pilgrims	**Enthroned on the praises of Israel.**
Officiant	In thee our fathers trusted;
Pilgrims	**They trusted, and thou didst deliver them.**

Psalm 22.1—4

RE PONDENS V
NIVE RSVS·POPVL VS
DIX T·SANGVIS·E IVS
SVPER NOS·ET·SVP ER
FILIOS NOSTROS·T VNC
DIMI SIT·ILLIS·BA RAB
BAM JESVM·AVT EM
FLAG ELLATVM·TR ADI
DIT EIS·VT·CRVC IFI
GE RETVR

1. JESUS IS CONDEMNED TO DEATH

Meditation

✠ ✠ ✠

Jesus is now, apparently, securely in the hands of the authorities, of officialdom, and distinctly at a disadvantage. Do we know a little something of this – though the consequences are never so terrible – when we are face to face with superior knowledge; with an authority greater than our own; with an impenetrable bureaucracy? But Jesus' responses to Pilate are quiet and assured.

How do we respond to our God-given vocation to be 'other Christs'? Do we respond in quiet assurance and absolute trust in God?

Between the columns of the portico are the words from St Matthew's Gospel to complete the scene shown in the carving. 'Then the people as a whole answered, "His blood be on us and on our children!" So he released Barabbas for them; and after flogging Jesus, he handed him over to be crucified.' (Matt. 27.25–26)

Pilate is seated rather grandly on a raised throne. However, he cannot look down upon Jesus: their eyes are at the same level. Is Pilate gazing sympathetically at Jesus and with respect; with, perhaps, an eagerness to know more, to talk further, to heed the words of his wife? Nevertheless, for the purposes of those who have brought Jesus to his court, he ceremonially washes his hands and declares himself innocent of Jesus' blood, his question 'What is truth?' still, perhaps, in the air.

Pilate's hands are together as they dip into the bowl of water, as surely bound as Jesus' hands. The robes flowing over the side in the manner of water spilling from the bowl partly obscure the text. Is Pilate failing the Roman constitution for the sake of expediency? Our sin too is many-layered.

Strengthen my faith, O Jesu, that I may say with the psalmist 'My God in whom I trust.'

I adore you, Lord Jesus, and bless you because by your Holy Cross you have redeemed the world.

✠

Deliver me, O Lord, from evil men; preserve me from violent men, who plan evil things in their heart, and stir up wars continually. They make their tongue sharp as a serpent's, and under their lips is the poison of vipers.

Psalm 140.1–3

✠

Officiant	Strengthen our faith, O Heavenly Father, that we may acknowledge with the psalmist 'Yet thou art holy . . . in thee our fathers trusted.' We adore you, O Christ, and we bless you;
Pilgrims	**Because by your Cross and precious Blood you have redeemed the world.**

✠

Officiant	Deliver me, O Lord, from evil men; preserve me from violent men;
Pilgrims	**Who plan evil things in their heart, and stir up wars continually.**
Officiant	They make their tongue sharp as a serpent's,
Pilgrims	**And under their lips is the poison of vipers.**

Psalm 140.1–3

II

JESUS RECEIVES HIS CROSS

✠
✠ ✠ ✠
✠

*For he will deliver you from the snare of the enemy, and from the deadly
pestilence; he will cover you with his pinions, and under his wings you will
find refuge; his faithfulness is a shield and buckler.*

Psalm 91.3–4

✠

Officiant	To thee they cried, and were saved;
Pilgrims	**In thee they trusted, and were not disappointed.**
Officiant	But I am a worm, and no man;
Pilgrims	**Scorned by men, and despised by the people.**

Psalm 22.5–6

II. JESUS RECEIVES HIS CROSS

Meditation

✠ ✠ ✠

The time has come to execute the sentence passed by Pilate. It begins here and now because before Jesus is killed on the cross, he first must be paraded from the city to Golgotha carrying the instrument of his death.

Jesus begins to shoulder the weight of his cross. The artist pictures two young men lowering the beam onto its victim; together these men might represent the whole of mankind offloading its burden of sin.

Jesus does not curse these men but accepts the burden with a backwards glance full of the Father's generous love.

Suddenly it is brought home to us that Jesus takes our sin upon him willingly, and shoulders our burden without demur.

How hurt and put upon we feel when others seem to place unreasonable burdens upon our shoulders. And how hard done by we feel when we are not thanked effusively and thanked again when we reluctantly offer or agree to perform some minor and insignificant task or other.

Society is divided by sin: the cross draws a diagonal line and divides the carving. Jesus is about to struggle away with the cross, leaving mankind without the terrible consequences of sin.

Do we appreciate the sheer joy of this fact? Do we understand?

I know the faithfulness of the Father, that it is my shield and buckler. May he know my faith and faithfulness. O Jesu, have mercy.

I adore you, Lord Jesus, and bless you because by your Holy Cross you have redeemed the world.

✠

Guard me, O Lord, from the hands of the wicked; preserve me from violent men, who have planned to trip up my feet. Arrogant men have hidden a trap for me, and with cords they have spread a net, by the wayside they have set snares for me.

Psalm 140.4–5

✠

Officiant	O Heavenly Father, your Son was laughed at in his misery; in the very act of taking away our sin. We adore you, O Christ, and we bless you;
Pilgrims	**Because by your Cross and precious Blood you have redeemed the world.**

✠

Officiant	Guard me, O Lord, from the hands of the wicked;
Pilgrims	**Preserve me from violent men, who have planned to trip up my feet.**
Officiant	Arrogant men have hidden a trap for me,
Pilgrims	**And with cords they have spread a net, by the wayside they have set snares for me.**

Psalm 140.4–5

III

JESUS FALLS THE FIRST TIME

✠
✠ ✠ ✠
✠

You will not fear the terror of the night, nor the arrow that flies by day, nor the pestilence that stalks in the darkness, nor the destruction that wastes at noonday.

Psalm 91.5–6

✠

Officiant	All who see me mock at me,
Pilgrims	**They make mouths at me, they wag their heads;**
Officiant	He committed his cause to the Lord; let him deliver him,
Pilgrims	**Let him rescue him, for he delights in him.**

Psalm 22.7–8

III. JESUS FALLS THE FIRST TIME

Meditation

✠ ✠ ✠

With his eyes set resolutely upon his destination, Jesus stumbles and falls to his knees. His human frame is tested to the extreme. He is facing the spears and the torments, the jostling, the mocking. Indeed, has the soldier caused him to stumble by increasing the weight of the cross? Certainly a soldier (is he a centurion, a sergeant-major?) is now cruelly pressing his knee against the cross in order to heighten the fun he is having at Jesus' expense, and to intensify his victim's humiliation. Jesus tries to struggle to his feet.

Do we suffer with fortitude and good grace or with complaint and bitterness towards those we suspect of having a hand in our circumstances?

Jesus is still clutching the cross: he has no doubts about the completion of his mission even if time and every step exacerbates his burden and increases his exhaustion.

Are we resolute? How easily do we despair of ourselves? Do we too readily concede defeat?

O Jesu, help me to trust and not to despair at the arrows that fly by day or the pestilence that stalks in darkness.

I adore you, Lord Jesus, and bless you because by your Holy Cross you have redeemed the world.

✠

I say to the Lord, Thou art my God; give ear to the voice of my supplications, O Lord! O Lord, my Lord, my strong deliverer, thou hast covered my head in the day of battle. Grant not, O Lord, the desires of the wicked; do not further his evil plot!

Psalm 140.6–8

✠

Officiant	O Heavenly Father, faithful to your will, Jesus accepted his mission while we jeered with the crowd at his discomfort. We adore you, O Christ, and we bless you;
Pilgrims	**Because by your Cross and precious Blood you have redeemed the world.**

✠

Officiant	I say to the Lord, Thou art my God;
Pilgrims	**Give ear to the voice of my supplications, O Lord!**
Officiant	O Lord, my Lord, my strong deliverer,
Pilgrims	**Thou hast covered my head in the day of battle.**
Officiant	Grant not, O Lord, the desires of the wicked;
Pilgrims	**Do not further his evil plot!**

Psalm 140.6–8

IV

JESUS MEETS HIS MOTHER

✠
✠ ✠ ✠
✠

A thousand may fall at your side, ten thousand at your right hand; but it will not come near you. You will only look with your eyes and see the recompense of the wicked. Because you have made the Lord your refuge, the Most High your habitation, no evil shall befall you, no scourge come near your tent.

Psalm 91.7–10

✠

Officiant	Yet thou art he who took me from the womb;
Pilgrims	**Thou didst keep me safe upon my mother's breasts.**
Officiant	Upon thee was I cast from my birth,
Pilgrims	**And since my mother bore me thou hast been my God.**

Psalm 22.9–10

IV. JESUS MEETS HIS MOTHER

Meditation

✠ ✠ ✠

What a contest of feelings is churning in the breast of Mary. She knew his path and hers, though not with any precision; after all, she had already said 'Yes, let it be so' thirty-odd years earlier. How might she wish to inhibit her Son's progress towards Golgotha; instead she receives his blessing.

There is resolution in Jesus' bold step forward and the carving recalls Gabriel's words to Mary 'Blessed are you among women' (Luke 1.28b), the prelude to Mary's own resolution.

How close on the heels of our resolutions and good intentions is our breaking point?

The soldier in charge of the rope, doubtless touched by the sorrowing mother, has permitted a momentary halt in the procession.

Are we even as responsive to others as this soldier?

May I, O Jesu, say yes without any regard for myself. Help me to make the Most High my habitation.

I adore you, Lord Jesus, and bless you because by your Holy Cross you have redeemed the world.

✠

Those who surround me lift up their head, let the mischief of their lips overwhelm them! Let burning coals fall upon them! Let them be cast into pits, no more to rise! Let not the slanderer be established in the land; let evil hunt down the violent men speedily!

Psalm 140.9–11

✠

Officiant	O Heavenly Father, Mary was there to greet your Son. She knew the joy of Bethlehem and the barrenness of Golgotha. May we be as resolute and steadfast. We adore you, O Christ, and we bless you;
Pilgrims	**Because by your Cross and precious Blood you have redeemed the world.**

✠

Officiant	Those who surround me lift up their head,
Pilgrims	**Let the mischief of their lips overwhelm them!**
Officiant	Let burning coals fall upon them!
Pilgrims	**Let them be cast into pits, no more to rise!**
Officiant	Let not the slanderer be established in the land;
Pilgrims	**Let evil hunt down the violent men speedily!**

Psalm 140.9–11

V

SIMON OF CYRENE HELPS JESUS TO CARRY THE CROSS

✠
✠ ✠ ✠
✠

For he will give his angels charge of you to guard you in all your ways. On their hands they will bear you up, lest you dash your foot against a stone.

Psalm 91.11–12

✠

Officiant	Be not far from me,
Pilgrims	**For trouble is near and there is none to help.**
Officiant	But thou, O Lord, be not far off!
Pilgrims	**O thou my help, hasten to my aid!**

Psalm 22.11–19

V. SIMON OF CYRENE HELPS JESUS
TO CARRY THE CROSS

Meditation

✠ ✠ ✠

The cross feels heavier with every step Jesus takes. His body has already been weakened by the beatings and by the crown of thorns. His back is raw; he squints through a raging headache. Now the soldier deputed to lead Jesus is out of sight but we know that he holds the rope around Jesus' waist. He has responded to the faltering footsteps behind and has enlisted a bystander to assist. Simon begins tentatively to take the tail of the cross, to clasp the wood and to place his feet in the footfall of Jesus.

We are called to take our modest crosses and follow Christ. Here Simon is assisting with Jesus' cross. We, too, whilst bearing our own burdens, are also called to assist in bearing the burdens of others. In doing so, we fulfil our general vocation to be 'other Christs'.

Simon and his family, along with many other pilgrims, have come to Jerusalem for the Passover. Simon's sons, Rufus and Alexander, survey the scene in some bewilderment; certainly the younger brother needs the comfort of a fraternal arm.

Do our feet step faithfully in the footfall of Jesus?

You, O Jesu, were strengthened by the way; may the Heavenly Father assist me when the going is difficult.

I adore you, Lord Jesus, and bless you because by your Holy Cross you have redeemed the world.

✠

I know that the Lord maintains the cause of the afflicted, and executes justice for the needy. Surely the righteous shall give thanks to thy name; the upright shall dwell in thy presence.

Psalm 140.12–13

✠

Officiant	O merciful Father, help us always to follow in the footsteps of your Son. We adore you, O Christ, and we bless you;
Pilgrim	**Because by your Cross and precious Blood you have redeemed the world.**

✠

Officiant	I know that the Lord maintains the cause of the afflicted,
Pilgrims	**And executes justice for the needy.**
Officiant	Surely the righteous shall give thanks to thy Name;
Pilgrims	**The upright shall dwell in thy presence.**

Psalm 140.12–13

VI

JESUS AND VERONICA

✠
✠ ✠ ✠
✠

You will tread on the lion and adder, the young lion and the serpent you will trample under foot. Because he cleaves to me in love, I will deliver him; I will protect him, because he knows my name.

Psalm 91.13–14

✠

Officiant	I will tell of my name to my brethren;
Pilgrims	**In the midst of the congregation I will praise thee.**
Officiant	For he has not despised or abhorred the affliction of the afflicted;
Pilgrims	**And he has not hid his face from him, but has heard, when he cried to him.**

Psalm 22.22–24

VI · JESUS AND VERONICA

Meditation

✠ ✠ ✠

With the soldier still in the lead, out of the picture and holding the rope, Veronica steps from the crowd, overcome with pity for the Master. She confronts him; her right foot meets his left. She is determined: she must do something for him no matter how small and seemingly insignificant.

Does Veronica here represent those women who followed him to Jerusalem from Galilee? Was she indeed the woman who was healed simply by touching the hem of his clothing during the early stages of his ministry?

Veronica risks the roughness of the other attendant soldiers to mop the blood and sweat from Jesus' forehead and from his eyes; to give what words of comfort she can, insignificant though she knows they will be. Jesus gratefully accepts this ministry, this gesture in its generous simplicity, but implores her not to linger, for her own safety.

Do we frequently resist the call to perform the simplest good deed? Are we gracious and humble enough to accept the simplest good deed ourselves?

O Jesu, your love for me is constant but my response is seldom as firm and as unequivocal as Veronica's. Help me.

I adore you, Lord Jesus, and bless you because by your Holy Cross you have redeemed the world.

✠

I call upon thee, O Lord; make haste to me! Give ear to my voice, when I call to thee! Let my prayer be counted as incense before thee, and the lifting up of my hands as an evening sacrifice!

Psalm 141.1—2

✠

Officiant	O Heavenly Father, help us to be receptive to others when they minister to us. We adore you, O Christ, and we bless you;
Pilgrims	**Because by your Cross and precious Blood you have redeemed the world.**

✠

Officiant	I call upon thee, O Lord; make haste to me!
Pilgrims	**Give ear to my voice when I call to thee!**
Officiant	Let my prayer be counted as incense before thee,
Pilgrims	**And the lifting up of my hands as an evening sacrifice!**

Psalm 141.1—2

VII

JESUS FALLS A SECOND TIME

✠
✠ ✠ ✠
✠

When he calls to me I will answer him; I will be with him in trouble, I will rescue him and honour him. With long life I will satisfy him, and show him my salvation.

Psalm 91.15–16

✠

Officiant	I am poured out like water, and all my bones are out of joint;
Pilgrims	**My heart is like wax, it is melted within my breast;**
Officiant	My strength is dried up like a potsherd, and my tongue cleaves to my jaws;
Pilgrims	**Thou dost lay me in the dust of death.**

Psalm 22.14–15

VII. JESUS FALLS A SECOND TIME.

Meditation

✠ ✠ ✠

Jesus' physical condition is wretched. He has fallen once already and the cross weighs heavily in spite of Simon's assistance. He stumbles again and falls to his knees. Simon is helpless, awkward; he is overcome by a mixture of emotions, embarrassed by his involvement, frightened that he might incur the wrath of the soldiers, worried that Rufus and Alexander might be lost or harmed, sorry for the victim he has been forced to help.

Jesus bows deeply under the weight of our sin and is forced into the most humble of postures, at the same time displaying the nobility of true humility. His physical attitude confirms that he is bending to the will of his Father; the cross is now his support and he clutches it almost as a faithful friend. The soldier displays a mixture of sympathy and impatience.

Are we embarrassed and awkward in the presence of those less fortunate than ourselves? Do we evince reluctant sympathy and dwindling patience?

O Jesu, your gift is everlasting life; prompt me when I fall short.

I adore you, Lord Jesus, and bless you because by your Holy Cross you have redeemed the world.

☩

Set a guard over my mouth, O Lord, keep watch over the door of my lips! Incline not my heart to do any evil, to busy myself with wicked deeds in company with men who work iniquity; and let me not eat of their pleasures.

Psalm 141.3–4

☩

Officiant   O Heavenly Father, help us to be mindful of those less fortunate than ourselves.
We adore you, O Christ, and we bless you;
Pilgrims   **Because by your Cross and precious Blood you have redeemed the world.**

☩

Officiant   Set a guard over my mouth, O Lord,
Pilgrims   **Keep watch over the door of my lips!**
Officiant   Incline not my heart to any evil, to busy myself with wicked deeds in company with men who work iniquity;
Pilgrims   **And let me not eat of their pleasures.**

Psalm 141.3–4

VIII

JESUS COMFORTS
THE WOMEN OF JERUSALEM

✠
✠ ✠ ✠
✠

*Rise up, O judge of the earth; render to the proud their deserts! O Lord,
how long shall the wicked, how long shall the wicked exult?*

Psalm 94.2–3

✠

Officiant	You who fear the Lord, praise him!
Pilgrims	**All you sons of Jacob, glorify him, and stand in awe of him, all you sons of Israel.**

Psalm 22.23

✠ JESUS DIXIT FILIAE JERUSALEM NOLITE FLERE SUPER ME SED SUPER VOS IPSAS FLETE ET SUPER FILIOS VESTROS QVONIAM ECCE VENIENT DIES IN QVIBUS DICENT BEA TAE STERILES & VENTRES

QVI NON GENU ERUNT ET UBERA QVAE NON LACTAVE RUNT

VIII. JESUS COMFORTS THE WOMEN OF JERUSALEM

Meditation

✠ ✠ ✠

The cross is resting on the ground and Simon is steadying it. Is the custody soldier turning a blind eye, or is it simply something of a tradition to allow this sort of encounter? But who were these women? Perhaps they were those who, by wailing loudly and wringing their hands, sought to prick the conscience of the condemned man. In the alternative, were they friends, acquaintances, or occasional followers? Were they among those who had followed Jesus from Galilee?

To these women Jesus says, 'Daughters of Jerusalem, do not weep for me, but weep for yourselves and for your children. For behold, the days are coming when they will say, "Blessed are the barren, and the wombs that never bore, and the breasts that never gave suck!"' (Luke 23.28b–29) And the artist cuts these words into the scene. Barrenness was always considered evidence of Divine displeasure. It is indeed a terrible prediction that there will come a time when the state of barrenness will be considered a blessed state. And does the address 'Daughters of Jerusalem' refer to the fact that these women were of the city of Jerusalem or is the address simply the feminine equivalent of 'Sons of Abraham'?

However, Jesus is merely citing many of the prophets of old and, like them, is pointing his listeners to the here and now. Indeed, he goes on to quote from the prophet Hosea: '. . . and they shall say to the mountains, "Cover us" and to the hills, "fall upon us".' For effect, he modifies the quotation slightly. Jesus strengthens the women by gently urging them to consider their own lives and predicaments. Are we fearful of looking too deeply into our own lives and our own spiritual needs?

*O Jesu, I know that in the Father's hands are all the issues; let me live
each day as though it were my last.*

*I adore you, Lord Jesus, and bless you because by your Holy Cross you
have redeemed the world.*

✠

*Let a good man strike me or rebuke me in kindness, but let the oil of the
wicked never anoint my head; for my prayer is continually against their
wicked deeds.*

Psalm 141.5

✠

Officiant	O Heavenly Father, we profess and call ourselves Christians: may we convince others by our very lives.
	We adore you, O Christ, and we bless you;
Pilgrims	**Because by your Cross and precious Blood you have redeemed the world.**

✠

Officiant	Let a good man strike or rebuke me in kindness,
Pilgrims	**But let the oil of the wicked never anoint my head; for my prayer is continually against their wicked deeds.**

Psalm 141.5

IX

JESUS FALLS A THIRD TIME

✠
✠ ✠ ✠
✠

They pour out their arrogant words, they boast, all the evildoers. They crush thy people, O Lord, and afflict thy heritage.

Psalm 94.4—5

✠

Officiant	Many bulls encompass me,
Pilgrims	**Strong bulls of Bashan surround me;**
Officiant	They open wide their mouths at me,
Pilgrims	**Like a ravening and roaring lion.**

Psalm 22.12—13

NE LAE-
TERIS.

INIMICA
MEA:

SUPER ME QVIA CECIDI
CONSURGAM:CUM SEDE
RO IN TENEBRIS
DOMINUS LUX
MEA EST.

IX JESUS FALLS A THIRD TIME

Meditation

✠   ✠   ✠

Overcome yet again by the weight of the cross as he nears Golgotha, Jesus falls once more. The main beam rakes his already bruised and bleeding back and, perhaps, adds a splinter to it as he falls badly. He is crushed and doubled-up. His left foot lands painfully, his toes out of joint. He grazes his knuckles on the stony path. The soldier is pushing at the arm of the cross in an effort to relieve Jesus of some of his burden. Simon, bewildered and wishing himself elsewhere, begins to raise the beam.

The quotation carved by the artist from the prophet Micah – 'Rejoice not over me, O my enemy; when I fall, I shall rise; when I sit in darkness, the Lord will be a light to me.' (Micah 7.8) – is apposite in isolation, but in context we hear the promise of the raising up of Israel despite her sin. We are reminded of the price of our sin. We can see its effect on Jesus. He can bend and stoop no lower. He is utterly humiliated beyond our imagining. The artist sees this scene as an acted parable about the descent of God into his creation, of God's stooping low in order to enter into our humanity.

Can we begin to understand just a little of the immensity of God's saving action?

It is easy, O Jesu, to see Godlessness in others; how often have I been the stony path upon which you have grazed your knuckles?

I adore you, Lord Jesus, and bless you because by your Holy Cross you have redeemed the world.

✠

When they are given over to those who shall condemn them, then they shall learn that the word of the Lord is true.

Psalm 141.6

✠

Officiant	O Heavenly Father, your Son suffered the burden of our sin, and as you raised him up you freed us from the evil one. Help us to believe in our hearts what we speak with our lips.
	We adore you, O Christ, and we bless you;
Pilgrims	**Because by your Cross and precious Blood you have redeemed the world.**

✠

Officiant	When they are given over to those who shall condemn them,
Pilgrims	**Then shall they learn that the word of the Lord is true.**

Psalm 141.6

X

JESUS IS STRIPPED OF
HIS CLOTHES

✠
✠ ✠ ✠
✠

*They shall slay the widow and the sojourner, and murder the fatherless;
and they shall say, 'The Lord does not see; the God of Jacob does not
perceive.'*

Psalm 94.6–7

✠

Officiant	They divide my garments among them,
Pilgrims	**And for my raiment they cast lots.**

Psalm 22.18

DIVISE͜RVNT SIBI·VES͜TIMENTA
MEA·ET SV PER VESTEM
MEAM MISE RVM SORTEM

X JESUS IS STRIPPED OF HIS CLOTHES

Meditation

✠   ✠   ✠

The excruciating torture of the journey is over, though the body is still trembling from the hardly imaginable abuse it has suffered. Any relief is tempered by the knowledge that the body will soon suffer even more terrible punishment. First, however, more humiliation and mockery: now for a little amusement for some of the soldiery, a little entertainment for some of the crowd. Jesus is laid bare, made naked, accompanied by the inevitable catcalling from the crowd and raucous ribaldry of the soldiers. The carving shows that this is the moment for the soldiers' performance. They have centre stage and have perfected their routine over countless public displays. They are the stars of the show and today they are particularly well prepared having acquired the taste for the mockery of this particular prisoner when they dressed him in a soldier's cloak, counterfeiting a kingly robe, and pressed on his head a crown made from long, flexible, thorny twigs. Jesus' blinding headache has persisted ever since.

Naked, the Incarnate God entered into humanity: naked, Jesus now begins the final stage prior to his death.

The artist records that the psalmist, from an entirely different world (or was it?), has already prophetically painted this picture for us. Jesus is naked; his clothes are stolen and distributed among his mockers. 'They divide my garments among them, and for my raiment they cast lots.' (Ps 22.18)

At the bottom right hand corner of the carving, the dice invite us to join the general merriment. How often do we snatch up those dice? Remember, some of the soldiers and some of the crowd would, at first, have felt uneasy.

O Jesu, how often do I say 'The Lord does not see'? I sin with indifference, and humiliate you with ease. Have mercy.

I adore you, Lord Jesus, and bless you because by your Holy Cross you have redeemed the world.

✠

But my eyes are toward thee, O Lord God; in thee I seek refuge; leave me not defenceless! Keep me from the trap which they have laid for me, and from the snares of the evildoers

Psalm 141.8–9

✠

Officiant	O Almighty God, you stooped low to take human flesh. May we, too, humble ourselves and never take the inappropriate seat at table through our own conceit and pride. We adore you, O Christ, and we bless you;
Pilgrim	**Because by your Cross and precious Blood you have redeemed the world.**

✠

Officiant	But my eyes are toward thee, O Lord God;
Pilgrims	**In thee I seek refuge; leave me not defenceless!**
Officiant	Keep me from the trap which they have laid for me,
Pilgrims	**And from the snares of the evildoers!**

Psalm 141.8–9

XI

JESUS IS NAILED TO THE CROSS

✠
✠ ✠ ✠
✠

Understand, O dullest of the people! Fools, when will you be wise? He who planted the ear, does he not hear? He who formed the eye, does he not see? He who chastens the nations, does he not chastise?

Psalm 94.8–10

✠

Officiant	Yea, dogs are round about me;
Pilgrims	**A company of evildoers encircle me; they have pierced my hands and feet –**
Officiant	I can count all my bones –
Pilgrims	**They stare and gloat over me.**

Psalm 22.16–17

VIDEBUNT IN QVEM TRANS-
FIXERUNT

XI JESUS IS NAILED TO THE CROSS

Meditation

✠ ✠ ✠

One soldier stands, supported by his spear. He has seen it all before; yet is there sympathy in his eye and in the inclination of his head? Or is there simply indifference? Can it be Simon of Cyrene who has just responded to 'Hold that leg steady, someone!' shouted by the soldier who is deftly positioning Jesus' left hand? There is something aquiline in the angle of this soldier's head, as he surveys his prey. Whoever the reluctant assistant is, his face is suffused with agony as he gazes at Jesus. Is every one of us that reluctant assistant? There is no end to what men will do.

What is our attitude to the plight of others?

With these different reactions to the sight before them, 'They look on him whom they have pierced.' The artist cuts into the scene this sentence from the prophet Zechariah (quoted in John 19.37b). John, however, gives this quotation after he records the piercing of Jesus' side. By anticipating this quotation is Gill saying to us 'Yes, and we shall pierce him again and again'?

After Jesus' hand is positioned, the soldier will kneel on the inside of the forearm and select a long iron nail. It will enter the hand at such an angle that the point will make its exit through the back of the wrist, and so into the wood of the cross.

How much do our sins wound him still? Can we imagine his pain and helplessness? Our hurts are as nothing.

O Jesu, of course you see all that I do; and often my doings are the nails that secure you to the tree.

I adore you, Lord Jesus, and bless you because by your Holy Cross you have redeemed the world.

✠

I cry with my voice to the Lord, with my voice I make supplication to the Lord. I pour out my complaint before him, I tell my trouble before him. When my spirit is faint, thou knowest my way!

Psalm 142.1–3

✠

Officiant   O Heavenly Father, how much do our sins
continue to wound your Son?
We adore you, O Christ, and we bless you;

Pilgrims   **Because by your Cross and precious Blood
you have redeemed the world.**

✠

Officiant   I cry with my voice to the Lord,
Pilgrims   **With my voice I make supplication to the Lord,**
Officiant   I pour out my complaint before him,
Pilgrims   **I tell my trouble before him.**
Officiant   When my spirit is faint,
Pilgrims   **Thou knowest my way!**

Psalm 142.1–3

XII

JESUS DIES UPON THE CROSS

✠
✠ ✠ ✠
✠

He who teaches men knowledge, the Lord, knows the thoughts of man that they are but a breath. If the Lord had not been my help, my soul would soon have dwelt in the land of silence.

Psalm 94.11–17

✠

Officiant   All the ends of the earth shall remember and
turn to the Lord;

Pilgrims   **And all the families of the nations shall
worship before him.**

Psalm 22.27

JESUS
DIXIT

CONSUM-
MATUM
EST

ET·VIDIMUS·EUM·ET·
NON·ERAT·ASPECTUS
VERE·LANGUORES

ET·DESIDERAVIMUS·EUM·
NOSTROS·IPSE·TULIT

XII JESUS DIES UPON THE CROSS

Meditation

✠   ✠   ✠

In his final effort to speak, Jesus gasps 'It is finished.' He bows his head and tastes death. These words are cut into the scene above the outpouring of his blood into Holy Church. The angel hovers with the chalice – the spear has now done its work – and makes the point with medieval simplicity. His death is indeed the consummation, and the Church is now to be nourished until our time and beyond, by his broken body and spilt blood.

The artist here raises us to a mystical plane: the closest witnesses – Mary and her nephew John (whom Jesus has recently made guardian and son to his mother) – are temporarily removed from the scene. We stand with them transported, gazing through our sadness at the majesty beyond the ruined body. Surely we now see that Jesus reigns from the cross as a king, and that this cross is none other than the Tree of Life itself. Without this tree there is no Consummation, no Resurrection, no Ransom, no Atonement, no Redemption, no Church.

In these circumstances what do we, there at his feet, say? And there at his feet the words from Isaiah II (Isaiah 53.2b, 4) are provided: 'And we have seen him, and there was no beauty that we should be desirous of him . . . Surely he has borne our griefs.'

O Jesu, when you breathed your last upon the cross and commended your spirit to the Father, you did so for me.

I adore you, Lord Jesus, and bless you because by your Holy Cross you have redeemed the world.

✠

I look to the right and watch, but there is none that takes notice of me; no refuge remains to me, no man cares for me. I cry to thee, O Lord; I say, thou art my refuge, my portion in the land of the living. Give heed to my cry; for I am brought very low!

Psalm 142.4–6a

✠

Officiant	O Heavenly Father, your Son was lifted high for our sake. What thanks do we give you? We adore you, O Christ, and we bless you:
Pilgrims	**Because by your Cross and precious Blood you have redeemed the world.**

✠

Officiant	I look to the right and watch, but there is none who takes notice of me;
Pilgrims	**No refuge remains to me, no man cares for me.**
Officiant	I cry to thee, O Lord;
Pilgrims	**I say, Thou art my refuge, my portion in the land of the living.**
Officiant	Give heed to my cry;
Pilgrims	**For I am brought very low!**

Psalm 142.4–6a

XIII

THE BODY OF JESUS IS TAKEN FROM THE CROSS AND LAID IN MARY'S BOSOM

✠
✠ ✠ ✠
✠

When I thought, 'My foot slips', thy steadfast love, O Lord, held me up.
When the cares of my heart are many, thy consolations cheer my soul.

Psalm 94.18–19

✠

Officiant　　Yea, to him shall all the proud of the earth
　　　　　　　bow down;
Pilgrims　　**Before him shall bow all who go down to the**
　　　　　　　dust, and he who cannot keep himself alive.

Psalm 22.29

XIII. THE BODY OF JESUS IS TAKEN FROM
THE CROSS AND LAID IN MARY'S BOSOM

Meditation

✠ ✠ ✠

The marks of the nails in the wood of the cross are transformed into stars and now represent and draw attention to the holy wounds themselves and sanctification of the cross. Both will become objects of devotion.

Under the direction of Joseph of Arimathea the lifeless body of Jesus is lowered from the cross. Is not the despair and disillusionment felt by Joseph, John and Mary palpable? Even so, does not Joseph reveal studied calm – a brave face – while the others are grief-stricken at their gruesome task?

Mary will now hold her son and weep for sadness as she held him at Bethlehem and there wept for joy.

Vegetation is springing up at the foot of the cross in anticipation of a new joy to come.

Can we raise guiltless eyes to this carving? And yet, we are redeemed!

O Jesu, in the arms of your mother at the foot of the cross what consolations then cheered her soul? She never wavered and was steadfast. Help me.

I adore you, Lord Jesus, and bless you because by your Holy Cross you have redeemed the world.

✠

Deliver me from my persecutors; for they are too strong for me! Bring me out of prison, that I may give thanks to thy name! The righteous will surround me; for thou wilt deal bountifully with me.

Psalm 142.6b–7

✠

Officiant   O Heavenly Father, there is grandeur here in the strength of a mother's love and in your love, which raises us up in the Resurrection of your Son.
We adore you, O Christ, and we bless you;

Pilgrims   **Because by your Cross and precious Blood you have redeemed the world.**

✠

Officiant   Deliver me from my persecutors;
Pilgrims   **For they are too strong for me!**
Officiant   Bring me out of prison, that I may give thanks to thy name!
Pilgrims   **The righteous shall surround me; for thou wilt deal bountifully with me.**

Psalm 142.6b–7

XIV

THE BODY OF JESUS IS LAID
IN THE TOMB

✠
✠ ✠ ✠
✠

They band together against the life of the righteous, and condemn the innocent to death. But the Lord has become my stronghold, and my God the rock of my refuge.

Psalm 94.21—22

✠

Officiant	Posterity shall serve him;
Pilgrims	**Men shall tell of the Lord to the coming generation,**
Officiant	And proclaim his deliverance to a people yet unborn,
Pilgrims	**That he has wrought it.**

Psalm 22.30—31

VENIT·HORA·UT·CLARIFICETUR·FILIUS·HO — MINIS

AMEN·AMEN
DICO·VOBIS
NISI· GRA-
NUM·FRU-
MENTI·CAD-
ENS·IN·TER-
RAM·MORTU-
UM·FUERIT
IPSUM·SOLŪ
MANET·SI·
AUTEM
MORTUŪ
FUERIT
MULTUM
FRUCTUM
AFFERT·

QVI·AMAT·ANIMAM·SUAM
PERDET·EAM·ET·QVI·ODIT
ANIMAM·SUAM·IN·HOC
MUNDO·IN·VITAM·AETER-
NAM·CUSTODIT·EAM

XIV THE BODY OF JESUS IS LAID IN THE TOMB

Meditation

✠   ✠   ✠

The lifeless body taken from the cross is rigid in death. The fingers of Jesus' right hand are fixed in the manner he would hold them to pronounce a blessing, anticipating blessings to come and recalling, perhaps, the fourth station in which he blessed his mother. From now on he will bless us all with the sign of his cross.

His body is to be laid in a place generously made available by his secret disciple, Joseph of Arimathea. The sorry procession enters the coolness and darkness to the echo of Jesus' own words: 'The hour has come for the Son of Man to be glorified. Truly, truly, I say to you, unless a grain of wheat falls into the earth and dies, it remains alone; but if it dies, it bears much fruit.' (John 12.23b–24) The words are there in the very fabric of the tomb.

Laid to rest are our sins and the sins of the whole world borne by Jesus in his Passion.

How stiff and unrelenting is our character? Do we exude the joy that is a life in Christ? All we have to do is to turn again.

Jesus' body is laid upon the stone bed of the tomb; perhaps this stone is reminiscent of Pilate's seat of judgement? The cloth drapes itself temporarily over the corner but only as the body is gently set down. No one observes the words as they continue: 'He who loves his life loses it, and he who hates his life in this world will keep it for eternal life.' (John 12.25) They are there for our benefit: they are there to point us to that which ought to be the object of our lives. This is indeed the throne from which Jesus will rise.

Let my meditations, O Jesu, spur me on to follow in your way without demur.

I adore you, Lord Jesus, and bless you because by your Holy Cross you have redeemed the world.

✠

[I will extol thee, my God and King, and bless thy name for ever and ever. Every day I will bless thee, and praise thy name for ever and ever.

Psalm 145.1–2]
(Used only if Station XV is to be prayed)

✠

Officiant	O Heavenly Father, it was from this cold and sorrowful place that your Son burst forth triumphant over the evil one.
	We adore you, O Christ, and we bless you;
Pilgrims	**Because by your Cross and precious Blood you have redeemed the world.**

✠

[Officiant	I will extol thee, my God and King,
Pilgrims	**And bless thy name for ever and ever.**
Officiant	Every day I will bless thee,
Pilgrims	**And praise thy name for ever and ever.**

Psalm 145.1–2]
(Used only if Station XV is to be prayed)

XV

[JESUS RISES FROM THE DEAD

✠
✠ ✠ ✠
✠

O sing to the Lord a new song; sing to the Lord, all the earth! Sing to the Lord, bless his name; tell of his salvation from day to day. Declare his glory among the nations; his marvellous works among all the peoples!

Psalm 96.1–3

✠

Officiant	Who shall ascend the hill of the Lord?
Pilgrims	**And who shall stand in his holy place?**
Officiant	He who has clean hands and a pure heart,
Pilgrims	**Who does not lift up his soul to what is false, and does not swear deceitfully.**

✠

Officiant	Lift up your heads, O gates! And be lifted up, O ancient doors!
Pilgrims	**That the King of glory may come in.**
Officiant	Who is the King of glory?
Pilgrims	**The Lord, strong and mighty, the Lord, mighty in battle!**
Officiant	Lift up your heads, O gates! And be lifted up, O ancient doors!
Pilgrims	**That the King of glory may come in.**
Officiant	Who is this King of glory?
Pilgrims	**The Lord of hosts, he is the King of glory!**

Psalm 24.3, 4, 7–10

NON EST HIC: SURREXIT ENIM, SICUT DIXIT:
VENITE, ET VIDETE LOCUM UBI POSITUS ERAT
DOMINUS

Meditation

✠   ✠   ✠

It is dawn. The tomb is empty save for the linen cloths that formerly bound Jesus: the stone slab is no longer a resting place for that pitifully gaunt and rigid corpse, because God has done something new. Jesus carried the weight of our sin to Golgotha, and to death; now he is raised up from the dead, and in this mystery he redeems mankind and raises it to new life in him. Had the artist created a fifteenth station, would we now see cut into the surface of the stone bed: *'Non est hic: surrexit enim, sicut dixit: venite, et videte locum ubi positus erat Dominus.'* ('He is not here; for he has risen, as he said. Come, see the place where the Lord lay.' Matthew 28.6)?

The tears in an hysterical woman's eyes temporarily convert the sight of Jesus into the gardener, whose gently spoken 'Mary' restores her vision as she responds 'Rabboni!' Timid, hopeful men hurry to the tomb, see and believe. The world is turned upside down just as it was turned inside out at Bethlehem. Men on the way to Emmaus encounter the Risen Lord. They hear him in the Scripture and recognize him in person at the Eucharist. We too are beneficiaries of these lavish gifts.

Do we come close to comprehending God's generosity? If so, how do we contain our joy as we encounter Jesus in others; in our priests at mass; as he is revealed to us in Holy Scripture; as we find him in prayer; and as he gives himself to us in the Holy Sacrament of the Altar? Our joy must shine brightly from our faces enabling others always to catch glimpses of Christ himself.]

FINAL PRAYERS
FOR PERSONAL DEVOTION

✠
✠ ✠ ✠
✠

O Heavenly Father, who desired your Son to suffer death on the cross for us that you might cast out from us the power of the enemy, grant that we may ever live in the joy of Jesus' Resurrection. Through Jesus Christ our Saviour, who lives and reigns with you and the Holy Spirit, one God, world without end. Amen.

✠

O give thanks to the Lord, for he is good; his steadfast love endures for ever! [Alleluia, alleluia.]

Psalm 118.1

✠

Our Father, who art in heaven,
Hallowed be thy name.
Thy kingdom come.
Thy will be done on earth, as it is in heaven.
Give us this day our daily bread,
And forgive us our trespasses,
As we forgive those who trespass against us,
And lead us not into temptation,
But deliver us from evil. Amen.

✠

Hail Mary full of grace, the Lord is with thee: blessed art thou among women, and blessed is the fruit of thy womb, Jesus. Holy Mary, Mother of God, pray for us sinners, now and at the hour of our death. Amen.

[Glory be to the Father, and to the Son, and to the Holy Spirit. As it was in the beginning is now and ever shall be, world without end. Amen.]

FINAL PRAYERS
FOR PUBLIC DEVOTION

✠
✠ ✠ ✠
✠

Officiant and Pilgrims say together the Anima Christi

Soul of Christ, sanctify me.
Body of Christ, save me.
Blood of Christ, inebriate me.
Water from the side of Christ, wash me.
Passion of Christ, strengthen me.
O good Jesus, hear me.
Within thy wounds hide me.
Suffer me not to be separated from thee.
From the enemy defend me.
In the hour of my death call me.
And bid me come to thee.
That with thy saints I may praise thee
For ever and ever. Amen.

✠

Officiant   O give thanks to the Lord, for he is good;
Pilgrims   **His steadfast love endures for ever!**
                [Alleluia, alleluia.]

Psalm 118.1

✠

Officiant   Let us pray:

O Heavenly Father who desired your Son to suffer death on the cross for us that you might cast out from us the power of the enemy, grant that we may ever live in the joy of Jesus' Resurrection. Through Jesus Christ our Saviour, who lives and reigns with you and the Holy Spirit, one God, world without end. **Amen.**

✠

Officiant and Pilgrims say together the Paternoster

Our Father, who art in heaven,
Hallowed be thy name.
Thy kingdom come.
Thy will be done on earth, as it is in heaven.
Give us this day our daily bread,
And forgive us our trespasses,
As we forgive those who trespass against us,
And lead us not into temptation,
But deliver us from evil. Amen.

✠

Officiant   Hail Mary full of grace, the Lord is with thee:
blessed art thou among women, and blessed is
the fruit of thy womb, Jesus.
Pilgrims   **Holy Mary, mother of God, pray for us sinners,**
now and at the hour of our death. Amen.

✠

[*Officiant*   Glory be to the Father, and to the Son, and to
the Holy Spirit.
Pilgrims   **As it was in the beginning is now and ever**
shall be, world without end. Amen.]

PART 2
STATIONS OF THE CROSS
FOR PERSONAL AND
PUBLIC DEVOTION

Using the stations provided in church

(The text in italics before and after the meditations is for the use of the private pilgrim)

✠
✠ ✠ ✠
✠
✠

PREPARATION
FOR PERSONAL DEVOTION

✠
✠ ✠ ✠
✠

+ *In the name of the Father, and of the Son, and of the Holy Spirit. Amen.*

O Lord Jesus, have mercy upon me and upon your whole Church living and departed. As I trace and meditate on the Way of the Cross, may I share in the merits of your Passion and may my heart be touched with sorrow and repentance that I may be ready to embrace with joy the sufferings and humiliations in my life and pilgrimage.

O Lord, come to me and help me.

[Glory be to the Father, and to the Son, and to the Holy Spirit. As it was in the beginning is now and ever shall be, world without end. Amen.]

PREPARATION
FOR PUBLIC DEVOTION

✠
✠ ✠ ✠
✠

Officiant + In the name of the Father, and of the Son, and of the Holy Spirit.

Pilgrims **Amen.**

Officiant O Lord Jesus have mercy upon us and upon your whole Church living and departed. As we trace and meditate on the Way of the Cross, may we share in the merits of your Passion and may our hearts be touched with sorrow and repentance that we may be ready to embrace with joy the sufferings and humiliations in our lives and pilgrimage. O Lord come to us,

Pilgrims **And help us.**

[*Officiant* Glory be to the Father, and to the Son, and to the Holy Spirit.

Pilgrims **As it was in the beginning is now and ever shall be, world without end. Amen.]**

The following may be said or sung (a suitable melody is provided)

At the Cross her station keeping
Stood the mournful Mother weeping,
Close to Jesus to the last.

At the first Station
JESUS IS CONDEMNED TO DEATH

✠
✠ ✠ ✠
✠

He who dwells in the shelter of the Most High, who abides in the shadow of the Almighty, will say to the Lord, 'My refuge and my fortress; my God, in whom I trust.'

Psalm 91.1–2

✠

Officiant	He who dwells in the shelter of the Most High, who abides in the shadow of the Almighty, will say to the Lord,
Pilgrims	**My refuge and my fortress; my God, in whom I trust.**

Psalm 91.1–2

Meditation

✠ ✠ ✠

Jesus stands before Pilate; there through envy and fear; there because we are in the crowd baying for blood and for the release of Barabbas. This is a fine irony because Jesus is to take the place of Barabbas (who is our representative) and pay the price of our sin. Those who bay for blood are those who will be saved by that very blood.

Perhaps we do not remain in that crowd: perhaps we simply run from the scene while Pilate, though fascinated by Jesus and loath to condemn him, washes his hands as the crowd eagerly accepts responsibility on our behalf.

O Jesu, with wonderful submission for my sake, you were condemned to die for my deceits, blasphemies and evil deeds.

I adore you, Lord Jesus, and bless you because by your Holy Cross you have redeemed the world.

✠

Arise, cry out in the night, at the beginning of the watches! Pour out your heart like water before the presence of the Lord! Lift your hand to him for the lives of your children, who faint for hunger at the head of every street.

Lamentations 2.19

✠

Officiant	O Jesu, with wonderful submission for our sake, you were condemned to die for our deceits, blasphemies and evil deeds. We adore you, O Christ, and we bless you;
Pilgrims	**Because by your Cross and precious Blood you have redeemed the world.**

✠

Officiant	Deliver me, O Lord, from evil men;
Pilgrims	**Preserve me from violent men, who plan evil things in their heart, and stir up wars continually.**
Officiant	They make their tongue as a serpent's,
Pilgrims	**And under their lips is the poison of vipers.**

Psalm 140.1–3

✠

The following may be said or sung

Through her heart, his sorrow sharing,
All his bitter anguish bearing,
Now at length the sword has passed.

At the second Station
JESUS RECEIVES THE CROSS

✠
✠ ✠ ✠
✠

*For he will deliver you from the snare of the enemy, and from the deadly
pestilence; he will cover you with his pinions, and under his wings you will
find refuge; his faithfulness is a shield and buckler.*

Psalm 91.3–4

✠

Officiant	For he will deliver you from the snare of the enemy, and from the deadly pestilence;
Pilgrims	**He will cover you with his pinions, and under his wings you will find refuge; his faithfulness is a shield and buckler.**

Psalm 91.3–4

Meditation

✠   ✠   ✠

By the time Jesus receives his cross he has been mocked in robe and crown of thorns, and soundly whipped. The cross is lowered over his shoulder and onto his bruised and bleeding back. The wounds around his head are causing a raging headache, which will continue until his dying gasp. He can but squint. These are the effects of man's sin now to be borne away by Jesus to Golgotha.

He staggers like a drunken man – doubtless the crowd finds this amusing – as he tries to adjust to the weight of the cross. He finds he has little control over his limbs.

O Jesu, by virtue of your Cross and Passion, grant that I may cheerfully
accept the trials and difficulties of my earthly pilgrimage.

I adore you, Lord Jesus, and bless you because by your Holy Cross you
have redeemed the world.

✠

I am a man who has seen affliction under the rod of his wrath; he has
driven and brought me into darkness without any light; surely against me
he turns his hand again and again the whole day long.

Lamentations 3.1—3

✠

Officiant	O Jesu, by virtue of your Cross and Passion
	grant that we may cheerfully accept the trials
	and difficulties of our earthly pilgrimage.
	We adore you, O Christ, and we bless you;
Pilgrims	**Because by your Cross and precious Blood**
	you have redeemed the world.

✠

Officiant	Guard me, O Lord, from the hands of the wicked;
Pilgrims	**Preserve me from violent men, who have**
	planned to trip up my feet.
Officiant	Arrogant men have hidden a trap for me, and
	with cords they have spread a net,
Pilgrims	**By the wayside they have set snares for me.**

Psalm 140.4—5

✠

The following may be said or sung

Oh, how sad and sore distressed
Was that Mother highly blessed
Of the sole-begotten One.

At the third Station
JESUS FALLS

✠
✠ ✠ ✠
✠

You will not fear the terror by night, nor the arrow that flies by day, nor the pestilence that stalks in the darkness, nor the destruction that wastes at noonday.

Psalm 91.5–6

✠

Officiant	You will not fear the terror by night,
Pilgrims	**Nor the arrow that flies by day,**
Officiant	Nor the pestilence that stalks in the darkness,
Pilgrims	**Nor the destruction that wastes at noonday.**

Meditation

✠   ✠   ✠

It is not surprising that Jesus, weakened almost beyond endurance, is unable to keep his feet. He falls. Do soldiers roughly pull him to his feet? In any event, he is determined to complete his mission and has absolute confidence and trust in God the Father; his resolve is undiminished. Once on his feet again he can only lurch from one footfall to the next. Do we rush from the crowd, anxious to do something for him?

The custody soldier ponders the problem: he must do something if this crucifixion is to be completed within the allotted time.

O Jesu, for my sins you have the burden of the Cross and fall under its weight. May thoughts of your sufferings make me watchful against temptation.

I adore you, Lord Jesus, and bless you because by your Holy Cross you have redeemed the world.

✠

He has made my teeth grind on gravel, and made me cower in ashes; my soul is bereft of peace, I have forgotten what happiness is; so I say, 'Gone is my glory, and my expectation from the Lord.'

Lamentations 3.16–18

✠

Officiant	O Jesu, for our sins you have the burden of the Cross and fall under its weight. May thoughts of your sufferings make us watchful against temptation. We adore you, O Christ, and we bless you;
Pilgrims	**Because by your Cross and precious Blood you have redeemed the world.**

✠

Officiant	I say to the Lord, Thou art my God;
Pilgrims	**Give ear to the voice of my supplications, O Lord!**
Officiant	O Lord, my Lord, my strong deliverer,
Pilgrims	**Thou hast covered my head in the day of battle.**
Officiant	Grant not, O Lord, the desires of the wicked;
Pilgrims	**Do not further his evil plot!**

Psalm 140.6–8

✠

The following may be said or sung

Christ above in torment hangs;
She beneath beholds the pangs
Of her dying glorious Son.

At the fourth Station
JESUS MEETS MARY

✠
✠ ✠ ✠
✠

A thousand may fall at your side, ten thousand at your right hand; but it will not come near you. You will only look with your eyes and see the recompense of the wicked. Because you have made the Lord your refuge, the Most High your habitation, no evil shall befall you, no scourge come near your tent.

Psalm 91.7–10

✠

Officiant	A thousand may fall at your side, ten thousand at your right hand;
Pilgrims	**But it will not come near you.**
Officiant	You will only look with your eyes
Pilgrims	**And see the recompense of the wicked.**
Officiant	Because you have made the Lord your refuge, the Most High your habitation,
Pilgrims	**No evil shall befall you, no scourge come near your tent.**

Psalm 91.7–10

Meditation

✠ ✠ ✠

There is respite of a sort. Perhaps it is the custody soldier who allows this temporary halt to enable the victim's mother to greet her son and he his mother. Perhaps this picture tells us something else. Mary realizes that this is part of her obedient 'Yes, let it be so' uttered modestly thirty-odd years before. So with restraint Mary steps out of the accompanying crowd to give Jesus a final embrace to reassure him on his way.

Here, Mary and Jesus jointly show the meaning of the selfless acceptance of God's will, the essential ingredient in the mission that leads to the salvation of mankind. Does Jesus end the encounter with a blessing? Does the meeting end with an impatient yell from the custody soldier or from the centurion further back in this sorry procession?

O Jesu, you embraced and blessed your mother on your way to Golgotha; grant that I too may embrace her and always remember her steadfastness.

I adore you, Lord Jesus, and bless you because by your Holy Cross you have redeemed the world.

☩

The Lord is good to those who wait for him, to the soul that seeks him. It is good that one should wait quietly for the salvation of the Lord. It is good for a man that he bear the yoke in his youth.

Lamentations 3.25–27

☩

Officiant	O Jesu, you embraced and blessed your mother on your way to Golgotha; grant that we too may embrace her and always remember her steadfastness. We adore you, O Christ, and we bless you;
Pilgrims	**Because by your Cross and precious Blood you have redeemed the world.**

☩

Officiant	Those who surround me lift up their head,
Pilgrims	**Let the mischief of their lips overwhelm them!**
Officiant	Let burning coals fall upon them!
Pilgrims	**Let them be cast into pits, no more to rise!**
Officiant	Let not the slanderer be established in the land;
Pilgrims	**Let evil hunt down the violent man speedily!**

Psalm 140.9–11

☩

The following may be said or sung

Is there one who would not weep.
Whelmed in miseries so deep,
Christ's dear Mother to behold?

At the fifth Station
JESUS IS ASSISTED BY SIMON OF CYRENE

✠
✠ ✠ ✠
✠

For he will give his angels charge of you to guard you in all your ways. On their hands they will bear you up, lest you dash your foot against a stone.

Psalm 91.11–12

✠

Officiant   For he will give his angels charge of you to
          guard you in all your ways.
Pilgrims   **On their hands they will bear you up,
          lest you dash your foot against a stone.**

Psalm 91.11–12

Meditation

✠ ✠ ✠

Jesus finds movement increasingly difficult. His burden is aggravated by each and every step. The custody soldier decides he must act and hauls a bystander – probably an unwilling one – from the crowd to assist Jesus. What fear is felt by this man, Simon of Cyrene? He, along with many others, is visiting Jerusalem for the celebration of the Passover. Simon is picked because he is there, to hand. The soldier probably scarcely looked at him. Unwilling though he may be, Simon acts out before us what is our general vocation – to carry one another's burdens in accordance with Jesus' own entreaty.

O Jesu, you were assisted with your burden so that I might learn to bear the burdens of others in this life.

I adore you, Lord Jesus, and bless you because by your Holy Cross you have redeemed the world.

✠

I called on thy name, O Lord, from the depths of the pit; thou didst hear my plea, 'Do not close thine ear to my cry for help!' Thou didst come near when I called on thee; thou didst say, 'Do not fear!'

Lamentations 3.55–57

✠

Officiant	O Jesu, you were assisted with your burden so that we might learn to bear the burdens of others in this life.
	We adore you, O Christ, and we bless you;
Pilgrims	**Because by your Cross and precious Blood you have redeemed the world.**

✠

Officiant	I know that the Lord maintains the cause of the afflicted,
Pilgrims	**And executes justice for the needy.**
Officiant	Surely the righteous shall give thanks to thy name;
Pilgrims	**The upright shall dwell in thy presence**.

Psalm 140.12–13

✠

The following may be said or sung

**Can the human heart refrain
From partaking in her pain,
In that Mother's pain untold?**

91

At the sixth Station
JESUS MEETS VERONICA

✠
✠ ✠ ✠
✠

You will tread on the lion and adder, the young lion and the serpent you will trample under foot. Because he cleaves to me in love, I will deliver him; I will protect him, because he knows my name.

Psalm 91.13—14

✠

Officiant	You will tread on the lion and adder,
Pilgrims	**The young lion and the serpent you will trample under foot.**
Officiant	Because he cleaves to me in love, I will deliver him;
Pilgrims	**I will protect him, because he knows my name.**

Psalm 91.13—14

Meditation

✠ ✠ ✠

Now the procession suffers another hiatus. Veronica, a woman clearly much devoted to Jesus, rushes forward to give what comfort she can. She mops the blood and sweat from his forehead and eyes, affording him some relief. It is an exquisite moment; a widow's mite moment.

Is Jesus conscious of the fact that her intrusion is unlikely to be tolerated by the soldier? Does he thank her profusely but urge her to return to the crowd for the sake of her own safety? Does she linger, careless for her own security, basking in the joy of being of simple service to her master?

O Jesu, you accepted the ministrations of Veronica, help me always to be gracious and humble enough to accept what others do for me.

I adore you, Lord Jesus, and bless you because by your Holy Cross you have redeemed the world.

✠

My eyes will flow without ceasing, without respite, until the Lord from heaven looks down and sees; my eyes cause me grief at the fate of all the maidens of my city.

Lamentations 3.49–51

✠

Officiant	O Jesu, you accepted the ministrations of Veronica, help us always to be gracious and humble enough to accept what others do for us.
	We adore you, O Christ, and we bless you;
Pilgrims	**Because by your Cross and precious Blood you have redeemed the world.**

✠

Officiant	I call upon thee, O Lord; make haste to me!
Pilgrims	**Give ear to my voice, when I call to thee!**
Officiant	Let my prayer be counted as incense before thee,
Pilgrims	**And the lifting up of my hands as an evening sacrifice!**

Psalm 141.1–2

✠

The following may be said or sung

Bruised, derided, cursed, defiled,
She beheld her tender Child
All with bloody scourges rent;

At the seventh Station
JESUS FALLS AGAIN

✠
✠ ✠ ✠
✠

When he calls to me I will answer him; I will be with him in trouble, I will rescue him and honour him. With long life will I satisfy him, and show him my salvation.

Psalm 91.15–16

✠

Officiant	When he calls to me I will answer him;
Pilgrims	**I will be with him in trouble, I will rescue him and honour him.**
Officiant	With long life will I satisfy him,
Pilgrims	**And show him my salvation.**

Psalm 91.15–16

Meditation

✠　✠　✠

Alas, Simon's help is insufficient: Jesus falls once more. As he falls, the cross rakes across his back; Simon, perhaps, feels a curious mixture of sympathy for the prisoner and anxiety for his own well-being. Should he be blamed, what would be his punishment?

The weight of man's sin is overwhelming, but it is also the cause of Jesus' bending to the will of his Father and the reason for our very salvation made so clear in this acted parable.

O Jesu, you fall again under the weight of my sin, grant that I may ever strive to do the will of the Heavenly Father no matter the difficulties.

I adore you, Lord Jesus, and bless you because by your Holy Cross you have redeemed the world.

✠

Men dogged our steps so that we could not walk in our streets; our end drew near; our days were numbered; for our end had come.

Lamentations 4.18

✠

Officiant	O Jesu, you fall again under the weight of our sin, grant that we may ever strive to do the will of the Heavenly Father no matter the difficulties. We adore you, O Christ, and we bless you;
Pilgrims	**Because by your Cross and precious Blood you have redeemed the world.**

✠

Officiant	Set a guard over my mouth,
Pilgrims	**O Lord, keep watch over the door of my lips!**
Officiant	Incline not my heart to do any evil, to busy myself with wicked deeds in company with men who work iniquity;
Pilgrims	**And let me not eat of their pleasures.**

Psalm 141.3–4

✠

The following may be said or sung

For the sins of his own nation,
Saw him hang in desolation,
Till his Spirit forth be sent.

At the eighth Station
JESUS MEETS THE GRIEVING
WOMEN

✠
✠ ✠ ✠
✠

Rise up, O judge of the earth; render to the proud their deserts! O Lord, how long shall the wicked, how long shall the wicked exult?

Psalm 94.2–3

✠

Officiant	Rise up, O judge of the earth;
Pilgrims	**Render to the proud their deserts!**
Officiant	O Lord, how long shall the wicked,
Pilgrims	**How long shall the wicked exult?**

Psalm 94.2–3

Meditation

✠ ✠ ✠

And what of these women? Were they among Jesus' friends or simply those who wrung their hands at every execution? To these women Jesus speaks firmly. They must look to the prophets and to his own preaching and teaching and realize that they must weep for themselves and for the sorry state of mankind to whom God has given such great riches. The hour has come, they ought already to have prepared themselves, but there is still time because God has infinite patience with his creation.

Are we there among these wailing women, wallowing in superficial sentiment?

O Jesu, you strengthened the women of Jerusalem; may I not be blinded from the truth and significance of your Cross and Passion by sentiment and superficiality.

I adore you, Lord Jesus, and bless you because by your Holy Cross you have redeemed the world.

✠

What can I say to you, to what compare you, O daughter of Jerusalem? What can I liken to you, that I may comfort you, O virgin daughter of Zion? For vast as the sea is your ruin; who can restore you?

Lamentations 2.13

✠

Officiant   O Jesu, you strengthened the women of Jerusalem; may we not be blinded from the truth and significance of your Cross and Passion by sentiment and superficiality. We adore you, O Christ, and we bless you;

Pilgrims   **Because by your Cross and precious Blood you have redeemed the world.**

✠

Officiant   Let a good man strike me or rebuke me in kindness.
Pilgrims   **But let the oil of the wicked never anoint my head; For my prayer is continually against their wicked deeds.**

Psalm 141.5

✠

The following may be said or sung

O thou Mother! Fount of love!
Touch my spirit from above,
Make my heart with thine accord.

At the ninth Station
JESUS FALLS A THIRD TIME

✠
✠ ✠ ✠
✠

They pour out their arrogant words, they boast, all the evildoers. They crush thy people, O Lord, and afflict thy heritage.

Psalm 94.4–5

✠

Officiant	They pour out their arrogant words, they boast, all the evildoers.
Pilgrims	**They crush thy people, O Lord, and afflict thy heritage.**

Psalm 94.4–5

Meditation

✠   ✠   ✠

Jesus manages a few more steps only and suffers another crushing fall. Does Simon despair of himself? Does a soldier curse and cry out again even more angrily? Does he hold a leash tied to a girdle around Jesus' waist?

This fall is the gravest, the most devastating of the three. Our hurts are as nothing. But what do we see in this final fall? We see how low God the Father has to stoop in order to enter into humanity. He regarded man's fallen state so mercifully that he sent his Son to bear the weight of that fallen nature.

O Jesu, you fall yet again as the burden of your mission crushes your weakened body despite the help from Simon. May I have the foresight to realize the likely consequences of my sin.

I adore you, Lord Jesus, and bless you because by your Holy Cross you have redeemed the world.

✠

To crush under foot all the prisoners of the earth, to turn aside the right of a man in the presence of the Most High, to subvert a man in his cause, the Lord does not approve.

Lamentations 3.34–36

✠

Officiant	O Jesu, you fall yet again as the burden of your mission crushes your weakened body despite the help from Simon. May we have the foresight to realize the likely consequences of our sin. We adore you, O Christ, and we bless you;
Pilgrims	**Because by your Cross and precious Blood you have redeemed the world.**

✠

Officiant	When they are given over to those who shall condemn them,
Pilgrims	**Then they shall learn that the word of the Lord is true.**

Psalm 141.6

✠

The following may be said or sung

Make me feel as thou hast felt;
Make my soul to glow and melt
With the love of Christ my Lord.

At the tenth Station
JESUS IS STRIPPED

✠
✠ ✠ ✠
✠

They shall slay the widow and the sojourner, and murder the fatherless; and they shall say, 'The Lord does not see; the God of Jacob does not perceive.'

Psalm 94.6–7

✠

Officiant   They shall slay the widow and the sojourner,
            and murder the fatherless;
Pilgrims   **And they shall say, 'The Lord does not see;
            the God of Jacob does not perceive.'**

Psalm 94.6–7

Meditation

✠   ✠   ✠

The journey is now over but there is no relief. At Golgotha, much to the delight of many in the crowd, some of the soldiers perform a party piece – the ceremonial humiliation of the prisoner. They strip him. He is laid bare. The scene pictures again for us God's descent into humanity, accompanied at Jesus' birth by the rudeness of the stable and rustic hospitality, and now by catcalls and ribaldry.

Jesus is as helpless as at birth. Are we there, enjoying Jesus' discomfiture?

O Jesu, you were humiliated for me and made as naked as you were at Bethlehem. May I not clothe myself with the distractions of this life as I try to fulfil my vocation to follow you.

I adore you, Lord Jesus, and bless you because by your Holy Cross you have redeemed the world.

✠

Thou hast heard their taunts, O Lord, all their devices against me. The lips and thoughts of my assailants are against me all the day long. Behold their sitting and rising; I am the burden of their songs.

Lamentations 3.61–63

✠

Officiant	O Jesu, you were humiliated for us and made as naked as you were at Bethlehem. May we not clothe ourselves with the distractions of this life as we try to fulfil our vocation to follow you. We adore you, O Christ, and we bless you;
Pilgrims	**Because by your Cross and precious Blood you have redeemed the world.**

✠

Officiant	But my eyes are toward thee, O Lord God;
Pilgrims	**In thee I seek refuge; leave me not defenceless!**
Officiant	Keep me from the trap, which they have laid for me,
Pilgrims	**And from the snares of the evildoers!**

Psalm 141.8–9

✠

The following may be said or sung

Holy Mother, pierce me through;
In my heart each wound renew
Of my Saviour crucified.

At the eleventh Station
JESUS IS NAILED TO THE CROSS

☩
☩ ☩ ☩
☩

Understand, O dullest of the people! Fools, when will you be wise? He who planted the ear, does he not hear? He who formed the eye, does he not see? He who chastens the nations, does he not chastise?

Psalm 94.8–10

☩

Officiant	Understand, O dullest of the people!
Pilgrims	**Fools, when will you be wise?**
Officiant	He who planted the ear, does he not hear?
Pilgrims	**He who formed the eye, does he not see?**
Officiant	He who chastens the nations,
Pilgrims	**Does he not chastise?**

Psalm 94.8–10

Meditation

✠ ✠ ✠

With deftness and, perhaps, an unhealthy fascination for his work, the appointed person fixes Jesus to the cross – man's wickedness securely bound to the fate of Jesus. And man's hope is pinned to the cross with the piercing of Jesus' hands and feet.

Mary and her nephew, John, watch this act of destruction. In their sadness can they see beyond? No, their sorrow is part of Jesus' Passion. A few friends look on with Mary and John. Are we there? Have we sheepishly returned to the scene?

O Jesu, you were crucified for my salvation yet my sin continues to pierce your hands and feet and side.

I adore you, Lord Jesus, and bless you because by your Holy Cross you have redeemed the world.

✠

Is it nothing to you, all you who pass by? Look and see if there is any sorrow like my sorrow, which was brought upon me.

Lamentations 1.12a

✠

Officiant	O Jesu, you were crucified for our salvation yet our sin continues to pierce your hands and feet and side. We adore you, O Christ, and we bless you;
Pilgrims	**Because by your Cross and precious Blood you have redeemed the world.**

✠

Officiant	I cry with my voice to the Lord,
Pilgrims	**With my voice I make supplication to the Lord.**
Officiant	I pour out my complaint before him.
Pilgrims	**I tell my trouble before him.**
Officiant	When my spirit is faint,
Pilgrims	**Thou knowest my way.**

Psalm 142.1–3

✠

The following may be said or sung

Let me share with thee his pain
Who for all my sins was slain,
Who for me in torments died.

At the twelfth Station
JESUS DIES ON THE CROSS

✠
✠ ✠ ✠
✠

He who teaches men knowledge, the Lord, knows the thoughts of man that they are but a breath. If the Lord had not been my help, my soul would soon have dwelt in the land of silence.

Psalm 94.11, 17

✠

Officiant	He who teaches men knowledge,
Pilgrims	**The Lord, knows the thoughts of man that they are but a breath.**
Officiant	If the Lord had not been my help,
Pilgrims	**My soul would soon have dwelt in the land of silence.**

Psalm 94.11, 17

Meditation

✠   ✠   ✠

As this pathetic body twisted in agony gasps 'It is finished!' we know that the pain is over; we know too by 'It is accomplished!' Jesus' mission is fulfilled; and by 'It is consummated!' the Church is born, to be nurtured by his blood and broken body, now and always.

The mocking label on the top of the cross reveals the truth; Jesus reigns in majesty from the Tree of Life itself.

O Jesu, you embraced mankind as you hung on the Cross; may I always devoutly embrace that honoured Cross.

I adore you, Lord Jesus, and bless you because by your Holy Cross you have redeemed the world.

✠

He has made my flesh and my skin waste away, and broken my bones; he has besieged and enveloped me with bitterness and tribulation; he has made me dwell in darkness like the dead of long ago.

Lamentations 3.4–6

✠

Officiant	O Jesu, you embraced mankind as you hung on the Cross;
	may we always devoutly embrace that honoured Cross.
	We adore you, O Christ, and we bless you;
Pilgrims	**Because by your Cross and precious Blood you have redeemed the world.**

✠

Officiant	I look to the right and watch, but there is none that takes notice of me;
Pilgrims	**No refuge remains to me, no man cares for me.**
Officiant	I cry to thee, O Lord;
Pilgrims	**I say, thou art my refuge, my portion in the land of the living.**
Officiant	Give heed to my cry;
Pilgrims	**For I am brought very low!**

Psalm 142.4–6a

✠

The following may be said or sung

Let me mingle tears with thee,
Mourning him who mourned for me,
All the days that I may live:

At the thirteenth Station
THE BODY OF JESUS IS TAKEN DOWN FROM THE CROSS

✠
✠ ✠ ✠
✠

When I thought, 'My foot slips', thy steadfast love, O Lord, held me up.
When the cares of my heart are many, thy consolations cheer my soul.

Psalm 94.18–19

✠

Officiant	When I thought, 'My foot slips',
Pilgrims	**Thy steadfast love, O Lord, held me up.**
Officiant	When the cares of my heart are many,
Pilgrims	**Thy consolations cheer my soul.**

Psalm 94.18–19

Meditation

✠　✠　✠

And yet we must contemplate two more stages of blankness and bleakness. How numbed are Mary and John as they assist Joseph of Arimathea in the removal of Jesus' body from the cross? They scarcely believe the nightmare. John must from now on look after Mary as Jesus has made him her son and in so doing has gained for us that relationship.

However, the son born of Mary is now placed lifeless in her arms, and she weeps for sorrow as she wept for joy when she nursed him at Bethlehem.

O Jesu, you were taken from the cross only after you had remained there in order to complete your mission. May I too be resolute in order to fulfil my vocation.

I adore you, Lord Jesus, and bless you because by your Holy Cross you have redeemed the world.

✠

Remember my afflictions and my bitterness, the wormwood and the gall! My soul continually thinks of it and is bowed down within me. But this I call to mind, and therefore I have hope.

Lamentations 3.19–21

✠

Officiant	O Jesu, you were taken from the Cross only after you had remained there in order to complete your mission. May we too be resolute in order to fulfil our vocation. We adore you, O Christ, and we bless you;
Pilgrims	**Because by your Cross and precious Blood you have redeemed the world.**

✠

Officiant	Deliver me from my persecutors;
Pilgrims	**For they are too strong for me!**
Officiant	Bring me out of prison that I may give thanks to thy name!
Pilgrims	**The righteous will surround me; for thou wilt deal bountifully with me.**

Psalm 142.6b–7

✠

The following may be said or sung

By the Cross with thee to stay;
There with thee to weep and pray;
Is all I ask of thee to give.

At the fourteenth Station
THE BODY OF JESUS IS LAID
IN THE TOMB

✠
✠ ✠ ✠
✠

They band together against the life of the righteous, and condemn the innocent to death. But the Lord has become my stronghold, and my God the rock of my refuge.

Psalm 94.21–22

✠

Officiant   They band together against the life of the righteous,
Pilgrims   **And condemn the innocent to death.**
Officiant   But the Lord has become my stronghold,
Pilgrims   **And my God the rock of my refuge.**

Psalm 94.21–22

Meditation

✠ ✠ ✠

Jesus, in the final act of those close to him at the end, is placed in the tomb generously made available by Joseph of Arimathea. The body is set down on the flat stone surface within the cave, dressed only in headband and shroud reminding us of the swaddling cloth at Bethlehem and his manger bed.

This is an end of the journey. When shall our tears of sadness turn to tears of joy? The dismay of that dismal party of mourners is all embracing.

However, we are blessed; we see the journey in the light of the Resurrection, for we are Easter people.

*O Jesu, as your body was enclosed in the Holy Sepulchre, may I enclose you
within my heart so that others may see you revealed in my daily life.*

*I adore you, Lord Jesus, and bless you because by your Holy Cross you
have redeemed the world.*

✠

*[But thou, O Lord, dost reign for ever; thy throne endures to all
generations. Why dost thou forget us for ever, why dost thou so long forsake
us? Restore us to thyself, O Lord, that we may be restored.*

Lamentations 5.19–21]
(Used only if Station XV is to be prayed)

✠

Officiant	O Jesu, as your body was enclosed in the Holy Sepulchre, may we enclose you within our hearts so that others may see you revealed in our daily life. We adore you, O Christ, and we bless you;
Pilgrims	**Because by your Cross and precious Blood you have redeemed the world.**

✠

[Officiant	I will extol thee, my God and King,
Pilgrims	**And bless thy name for ever and ever.**
Officiant	Every day I will bless thee,
Pilgrims	**And praise thy name for ever end ever.**

Psalm 145.1–2]
(Used only if Station XV is to be prayed.)

✠

The following may be said or sung

While my body here decays,
May my soul Christ's goodness praise,
Safe in Paradise with him.

(tr. Edward Caswall 1814–78)

At the fifteenth Station
[JESUS RISES FROM THE DEAD

✠
✠ ✠ ✠
✠

*O sing to the Lord a new song; sing to the Lord, all the earth! Sing to the
Lord, bless his name; tell of his salvation from day to day. Declare his glory
among the nations; his marvellous works among all the peoples!*

Psalm 96.1–3

✠

Officiant   O sing to the Lord a new song;
Pilgrims   **Sing to the Lord, all the earth!**
Officiant   Sing to the Lord, bless his name;
Pilgrims   **Tell of his salvation from day to day.**
Officiant   Declare his glory among the nations;
Pilgrims   **His marvellous works among all the peoples!**

Psalm 96.1–3

Meditation

✠   ✠   ✠

With a sun-burst of pure energy, God does something new and turns the world upside down, as he turned it inside out at Bethlehem. The gaunt corpse is gone: it is raised up from the dead. Through Mary Magdalene's tears Jesus takes the appearance of the gardener. The tears clear as soon as her name is spoken, and she knows and sees the Risen Lord.

Men run to the empty tomb, see and believe. Those on the way to Emmaus find Jesus in the word of Scripture and in person at the Eucharist. The fire has broken free and will burn brightly for ever.

O give thanks to the Lord, for he is good; his steadfast love endures for ever!
[Alleluia, alleluia.]

Psalm 118.1

✠

Officiant	O give thanks to the Lord, for he is good;
Pilgrims	**His steadfast love endures for ever!**
	[Alleluia, alleluia.]

Psalm 118.1

✠

The following may be said or sung

Christ, whose glory burning bright,
Bursts from tomb in blaze of light,
Breaks the bonds of death and sin.]

FINAL PRAYERS
FOR PERSONAL DEVOTION

✠
✠ ✠ ✠
✠

O Risen Lord, secure in me the knowledge of your forgiving mercy, the comfort of your redeeming love, and the joy of your all-powerful Resurrection from the dead. Give me the strength to take up my cross and follow you to the heavenly realms where you reign in glory with the Father and the Holy Spirit throughout all ages. Amen.

✠

Our Father, who art in heaven,
Hallowed be thy name.
Thy kingdom come.
Thy will be done on earth, as it is in heaven.
Give us this day our daily bread,
And forgive us our trespasses,
As we forgive those who trespass against us,
And lead us not into temptation,
But deliver us from evil. Amen.

✠

Hail Mary full of grace, the Lord is with thee: blessed art thou among women, and blessed is the fruit of thy womb, Jesus. Holy Mary, Mother of God, pray for us sinners, now, and at the hour of our death. Amen.

✠

[Glory be to the Father, and to the Son, and to the Holy Spirit. As it was in the beginning is now and ever shall be, world without end. Amen.]

FINAL PRAYERS
FOR PUBLIC DEVOTION

✠
✠ ✠ ✠
✠

Officiant   O Risen Lord, secure in us the knowledge of your forgiving mercy, the comfort of your redeeming love, and
the joy of your all-powerful Resurrection from the
dead. Give us the strength to take up our crosses and
follow you to the heavenly realms where you reign in
glory with the Father and the Holy Spirit throughout all
ages.

Pilgrims   **Amen.**

✠

Officiant and Pilgrims say together the Paternoster

Our Father, who art in heaven,
Hallowed be thy name.
Thy kingdom come.
Thy will be done on earth, as it is in heaven.
Give us this day our daily bread,
And forgive us our trespasses,
As we forgive those who trespass against us,
And lead us not into temptation,
But deliver us from evil. Amen.

✠

Officiant	Hail Mary full of grace, the Lord is with thee: blessed art thou among women, and blessed is the fruit of thy womb, Jesus.
Pilgrims	**Holy Mary, Mother of God, pray for us sinners, now, and at the hour of our death. Amen.**

✠

[*Officiant*	Glory be to the Father, and to the Son, and to the Holy Spirit.
Pilgrims	**As it was in the beginning is now and ever shall be, world without end. Amen.**]

APPENDIX
THE LATIN INSCRIPTIONS OF THE
ERIC GILL STATIONS

✠
✠ ✠ ✠
✠

I JESUS IS CONDEMNED TO DEATH

ET RESPONDENS UNIVERSUS POPULUS, DIXIT:
SANGUIS EIUS SUPER NOS, ET SUPER FILIOS
NOSTROS. TUNC DIMISIT ILLIS BARABBAM:
JESUM AUTEM FLAGELLATUM TRADIDIT EIS UT
CRUCIFIGERETUR

Then the people as a whole answered, 'His blood be on us and on
our children!' So he released Barabbas for them; and after flogging
Jesus, he handed him over to be crucified.

Matthew 27.25–26

SENATUS POPULUSQUE ROMANUS
The Roman Senate and People (SPQR)

II JESUS RECEIVES HIS CROSS
&
III JESUS FALLS THE FIRST TIME
Without inscription

IV JESUS MEETS HIS MOTHER

BENEDICTA TU IN MULIERIBUS
Blessed are you among women.
Luke 1.28b

V SIMON OF CYRENE HELPS JESUS TO
CARRY THE CROSS
VI JESUS AND VERONICA
&
VII JESUS FALLS A SECOND TIME
Without inscription

VIII JESUS COMFORTS THE WOMEN OF
JERUSALEM

JESUS DIXIT: (O) FILIAE JERUSALEM, NOLITE
FLERE SUPER ME, SED SUPER VOS IPSUS FLETE
ET SUPER FILIOS VESTROS. QUONIAM ECCE
VENIENT DIES IN QUIBUS DICENT; BEATAE
STERILES, ET VENTRES QUI NON GENUERUNT
ET UBEA QUAE NON LACTAVERUNT
Jesus said: 'Daughters of Jerusalem, do not weep for me, but weep
for yourselves and for your children. For behold, the days are
coming when they will say, "Blessed are the barren, and the
wombs that never bore, and the breasts that never gave suck!"'
Luke 23.28b–29

IX JESUS FALLS A THIRD TIME

NE LAETERIS, INIMICA MEA, SUPER ME, QUIA
CECIDI; CONSURGAM CUM SEDERO IN
TENEBRIS: DOMINUS LUX MEA EST
Rejoice not over me, O my enemy; when I fall, I shall rise; when I
sit in darkness, the Lord will be a light to me.
Micah 7.8

X JESUS IS STRIPPED OF HIS CLOTHES

DIVISERUNT SIBI VESTIMENTA MEA, ET SUPER VESTEM MEAM MISERUNT SORTEM

They divide my garments among them, and for my raiment they cast lots.

Psalm 22.19 [v.18 in the Biblia Vulgata]

XI JESUS IS NAILED TO THE CROSS

VIDEBUNT IN QUEM TRANSFIXERUNT

'They look on him whom they have pierced.'

John 19.37b, quoting Zechariah 12.10

XII JESUS DIES UPON THE CROSS

INRI (IESUS NAZARENUS REX IUDAEORUM)

Jesus of Nazareth King of the Jews.

John 19.19

JESUS DIXIT: CONSUMATUM EST

Jesus . . . said: 'It is finished.'

John 19.30b

ET VIDIMUS EUM, ET NON ERAT ASPECTUS, ET DESIDERAVIMUS EUM

And we have seen him, and there was no beauty that we should be desirous of him.

Isaiah 53.2b

VERE LANGUORES NOSTROS IPSE TULIT

Surely he has borne our griefs.

Isaiah 53.4

XIII THE BODY OF JESUS IS TAKEN FROM THE CROSS AND LAID IN MARY'S BOSOM

INRI (IESUS NAZARENUS REX IUDAEORUM)
Jesus of Nazareth King of the Jews
John 19.19

XIV THE BODY OF JESUS IS LAID IN THE TOMB

VENIT HORA, UT CLARIFICETUR FILIUS
HOMINIS. AMEN, AMEN DICO VOBIS, NISI
GRANUM FRUMENTI CADENS IN TERRAM,
MORTUUM FUERIT, IPSUM SOLUM MANET: SI
AUTEM MORTUUM FUERIT, MULTUM FRUCTUM
AFFERT. QUI AMAT ANIMAM SUAM, PERDET
EAM; ET QUI ODIT ANIMAM SUAM IN HOC
MUNDO, IN VITAM AETERNAM CUSTODIT EAM
'The hour has come for the Son of Man to be glorified. Truly,
truly, I say to you, unless a grain of wheat falls into the earth and
dies, it remains alone; but if it dies, it bears much fruit. He who
loves his life loses it, and he who hates his life in this world will
keep it for eternal life.'
John 12.23b–25

XV JESUS RISES FROM THE DEAD*

NON EST HIC: SURREXIT ENIM, SICUT DIXIT:
VENITE, ET VIDETE LOCUM UBI POSITUS ERAT
DOMINUS
'He is not here; for he has risen, as he said. Come and see the place
where the Lord lay.'
Matthew 28.6
* not included in the Gill Stations